EASY MUFFIN COOKBOOK

A MUFFIN BOOK FILLED WITH 50 DELICIOUS MUFFIN RECIPES

By
BookSumo Press
Copyright © by Saxonberg Associates

Published by
BookSumo Press, a DBA of Saxonberg Associates
http://www.booksumo.com/

ABOUT THE AUTHOR.

BookSumo Press is a publisher of unique, easy, and healthy cookbooks.

Our cookbooks span all topics and all subjects. If you want a deep dive into the possibilities of cooking with any type of ingredient. Then BookSumo Press is your go to place for robust yet simple and delicious cookbooks and recipes. Whether you are looking for great tasting pressure cooker recipes or authentic ethic and cultural food. BookSumo Press has a delicious and easy cookbook for you.

With simple ingredients, and even simpler step-by-step instructions BookSumo cookbooks get everyone in the kitchen chefing delicious meals.

BookSumo is an independent publisher of books operating in the beautiful Garden State (NJ) and our team of chefs and kitchen experts are here to teach, eat, and be merry!

INTRODUCTION

Welcome to *The Effortless Chef Series*! Thank you for taking the time to purchase this cookbook.

Come take a journey into the delights of easy cooking. The point of this cookbook and all BookSumo Press cookbooks is to exemplify the effortless nature of cooking simply.

In this book we focus on Muffins. You will find that even though the recipes are simple, the taste of the dishes are quite amazing.

So will you take an adventure in simple cooking? If the answer is yes please consult the table of contents to find the dishes you are most interested in.

Once you are ready, jump right in and start cooking.

— BookSumo Press

TABLE OF CONTENTS

ANY ISSUES? CONTACT US

If you find that something important to you is missing from this book please contact us at info@booksumo.com.

We will take your concerns into consideration when the 2nd edition of this book is published. And we will keep you updated!

— BookSumo Press

Legal Notes

COMMON ABBREVIATIONS

cup(s)	C.
tablespoon	tbsp
teaspoon	tsp
ounce	oz.
pound	lb

*All units used are standard American measurements

CHAPTER 1: EASY MUFFIN RECIPES

CRUMB NANA MUFFINS

Ingredients

- 1 1/2 C. all-purpose flour
- 1 tsp baking soda
- 1 tsp baking powder
- 1/2 tsp salt
- 3 bananas, mashed
- 3/4 C. white sugar
- 1 egg, lightly beaten
- 1/3 C. butter, melted
- 1/3 C. packed brown sugar
- 2 tbsp all-purpose flour
- 1/8 tsp ground cinnamon
- 1 tbsp butter

Directions

- Set your oven to 375 degrees F before doing anything else and lightly, grease 10 cups of a muffin pan.
- In a large bowl, mix together 1 1/2 C. of the flour, baking soda, baking powder and salt.
- In another bowl, add the bananas, sugar, egg and melted butter and beat till well combined.
- Add the banana mixture into the flour mixture and mix till just moistened.

- Transfer the mixture into the prepared muffin cups evenly.
- For topping in a small bowl, mix together the brown sugar, 2 tbsp of the flour and cinnamon.
- With a pastry cutter, cut 1 tbsp of the butter and mix till the mixture resembles to a coarse cornmeal.
- Sprinkle the topping over the muffins evenly.
- Cook in the oven for about 18-20 minutes or till a toothpick inserted in the center comes out clean.

Amount per serving (10 total)

Timing Information:

Preparation	15 m
Cooking	20 m
Total Time	35 m

Nutritional Information:

Calories	263 kcal
Fat	8.1 g
Carbohydrates	46g
Protein	3.2 g
Cholesterol	38 mg
Sodium	352 mg

* Percent Daily Values are based on a 2,000 calorie diet.

Baby's Muffins

Ingredients

- 1/2 C. butter, softened
- 1/2 C. brown sugar
- 2 large bananas, mashed
- 1 (4.5 oz.) jar baby food squash
- 2 carrots, grated
- 2 eggs, beaten
- 1 C. all-purpose flour
- 1/2 C. oat bran
- 1 tsp baking soda
- 1 tsp pumpkin pie spice
- 1/2 tsp salt

Directions

- Set your oven to 375 degrees F before doing anything else and grease 24 cups of the mini muffin pans.
- In a bowl, add the butter and brown sugar and beat till creamy and smooth.
- Add the mashed bananas, squash, carrots, and eggs and mix well.
- In another bowl, mix together the flour, oat bran, baking soda, pumpkin pie spice and salt.
- Add the flour mixture into butter mixture and mix till just combined.
- Transfer the mixture into the prepared muffin cups evenly.

- Cook in the oven for about 15-20 minutes or till a toothpick inserted in the center comes out clean.
- Remove from the oven and cool for about 10 minutes before turning out onto wire rack to cool completely.

Amount per serving (24 total)

Timing Information:

Preparation	15 m
Cooking	15 m
Total Time	30 m

Nutritional Information:

Calories	89 kcal
Fat	4.5 g
Carbohydrates	11.8g
Protein	1.6 g
Cholesterol	24 mg
Sodium	141 mg

* Percent Daily Values are based on a 2,000 calorie diet.

SIMPLE SUGAR MUFFINS

Ingredients

- 1 egg
- 1/2 C. milk
- 1/4 C. vegetable oil
- 1 1/2 C. all-purpose flour, sifted
- 1/2 C. white sugar
- 2 tsp baking powder
- 1/2 tsp salt

Directions

- Set your oven to 400 degrees F before doing anything else and grease 12 cups of a muffin pan.
- In a bowl, add the egg and beat with a fork.
- Stir in the milk and oil.
- In another bowl, mix together the sugar, baking powder and salt.
- Add the egg mixture into flour mixture and stir till the mixture is just moistened.
- Transfer the mixture into the prepared muffin cups about 2/3 full.
- Cook in the oven for about 20-25 minutes or till a toothpick inserted in the center comes out clean.

Amount per serving (12 total)

Timing Information:

Preparation	10 m
Cooking	20 m
Total Time	30 m

Nutritional Information:

Calories	141 kcal
Fat	5.4 g
Carbohydrates	21g
Protein	2.5 g
Cholesterol	16 mg
Sodium	188 mg

* Percent Daily Values are based on a 2,000 calorie diet.

WHOLE WHEAT MUFFINS

Ingredients

- 2 1/4 C. whole wheat flour
- 1/3 C. millet
- 1 tsp baking powder
- 1 tsp baking soda
- 1 tsp salt
- 1 C. buttermilk
- 1 egg, lightly beaten
- 1/2 C. vegetable oil
- 1/2 C. honey

Directions

- Set your oven to 400 degrees F before doing anything else and lightly, grease 10 cups of a muffin pan.
- In a large bowl, mix together the whole wheat flour, millet flour, baking powder, baking soda and salt.
- In another bowl, mix together the buttermilk, egg, vegetable oil and honey.
- Add the buttermilk mixture into the flour mixture and mix till just moistened.
- Transfer the mixture into the prepared muffin cups evenly.
- Cook in the oven for about 15 minutes or till a toothpick inserted in the center comes out clean.

Amount per serving (16 total)

Timing Information:

Preparation	10 m
Cooking	15 m
Total Time	25 m

Nutritional Information:

Calories	176 kcal
Fat	7.7 g
Carbohydrates	24.8g
Protein	3.7 g
Cholesterol	12 mg
Sodium	268 mg

* Percent Daily Values are based on a 2,000 calorie diet.

OCTOBER'S MUFFINS

Ingredients

- 3/4 C. brown sugar
- 3/4 C. white sugar
- 3 C. all-purpose flour
- 1/2 tsp baking soda
- 1 tbsp baking powder
- 1/2 tsp salt
- 2 tsp ground cinnamon
- 1/2 tsp ground nutmeg
- 1 tsp ground ginger
- 1 C. butter, melted
- 2 eggs, beaten
- 1 1/4 C. milk
- 1 C. chopped cranberries
- 1 C. chopped, peeled apple
- 1/2 C. chopped dried figs
- 3/4 C. chopped toasted hazelnuts

Directions

Set your oven to 375 degrees F before doing anything else and grease 18 cups of the muffin pans.

In a large bowl, mix together the brown sugar, white sugar, flour, baking powder, baking soda, salt, cinnamon, nutmeg and ginger.

Make a well in the center of the mixture.

In the well, add the melted butter, milk and eggs and mix till smooth.

Fold in the cranberries, apple, figs and hazelnuts.

Transfer the mixture into the prepared muffin cups about 3/4 full.

Cook in the oven for about 15-20 minutes or till a toothpick inserted in the center comes out clean.

Amount per serving (18 total)

Timing Information:

Preparation	45 m
Cooking	30 m
Total Time	1 h 15 m

Nutritional Information:

Calories	304 kcal
Fat	14.6 g
Carbohydrates	40.9g
Protein	4.2 g
Cholesterol	49 mg
Sodium	284 mg

* Percent Daily Values are based on a 2,000 calorie diet.

EASY ALMOND RHUBARB MUFFINS

Ingredients

- 1/2 C. vanilla yogurt
- 2 tbsp butter, melted
- 2 tbsp vegetable oil
- 1 egg
- 1 1/3 C. all-purpose flour
- 3/4 C. brown sugar
- 1/2 tsp baking soda
- 1/4 tsp salt
- 1 C. diced rhubarb
- 1/4 C. brown sugar
- 1/2 tsp ground cinnamon
- 1/4 tsp ground nutmeg
- 1/4 C. crushed sliced almonds
- 2 tsp melted butter

Directions

- Set your oven to 350 degrees F before doing anything else and lightly, grease 12 cups of a muffin pan.
- In a bowl, mix together the yogurt, 2 tbsp of the melted butter, oil and egg.
- In another large bowl, mix together the flour, 3/4 C. of the brown sugar, baking soda and salt.
- Add the yogurt mixture into the flour mixture and mix till just combined.
- Fold in the rhubarb.

- Transfer the mixture into the prepared muffin cups about 2/3 full.
- In a small bowl, mix together 1/4 C. of the brown sugar, cinnamon, nutmeg, almonds and 2 tsp of the melted butter.
- Place the mixture over the tops of the muffins and press down slightly.
- Cook in the oven for about 25 minutes or till a toothpick inserted in the center comes out clean.
- Remove from the oven and cool for about 15 minutes before turning out onto wire rack to cool completely.

Amount per serving (12 total)

Timing Information:

Preparation	10 m
Cooking	25 m
Total Time	35 m

Nutritional Information:

Calories	192 kcal
Fat	6.6 g
Carbohydrates	31g
Protein	3 g
Cholesterol	23 mg
Sodium	138 mg

* Percent Daily Values are based on a 2,000 calorie diet.

Ivy League Muffins

Ingredients

- 1 egg
- 1 1/3 C. mashed ripe banana
- 3/4 C. packed brown sugar
- 1/3 C. applesauce
- 1 tsp vanilla extract
- 1 C. all-purpose flour
- 1/2 tsp baking soda
- 2 tsp baking powder
- 1 1/4 tsp salt
- 1 tsp ground cinnamon
- 1 C. quick cooking oats
- 1/2 C. semisweet chocolate chips
- 1/2 C. chopped walnuts

Directions

- Set your oven to 350 degrees F before doing anything else and lightly, grease 12 cups of a muffin pan.
- In a large bowl, add the egg, banana, brown sugar, applesauce and vanilla and beat till well combined.
- In another bowl, sift together the flour, baking soda, baking powder, salt and cinnamon.
- Add the flour mixture and oatmeal into banana mixture and gently, stir to combine.
- Fold in the chocolate chips and walnuts.

- Transfer the mixture into the prepared muffin cups evenly.
- Cook in the oven for about 15-20 minutes or till a toothpick inserted in the center comes out clean.
- Remove from the oven and keep on wire rack to cool completely.

Amount per serving (12 total)

Timing Information:

Preparation	10 m
Cooking	20 m
Total Time	30 m

Nutritional Information:

Calories	215 kcal
Fat	6.4 g
Carbohydrates	38g
Protein	3.8 g
Cholesterol	18 mg
Sodium	366 mg

* Percent Daily Values are based on a 2,000 calorie diet.

WEDNESDAY'S MUFFINS

Ingredients

- 1 1/2 C. all-purpose flour
- 1 tsp baking powder
- 1 tsp baking soda
- 1/2 tsp salt
- 3 large bananas, mashed
- 3/4 C. white sugar
- 1 egg
- 1/3 C. butter, melted

Directions

- Set your oven to 350 degrees F before doing anything else and lightly, grease 12 cups of a muffin pan.
- In a bowl, sift together the flour, baking powder, baking soda and salt.
- In another large bowl, add the bananas, sugar, egg and melted butter and beat till well combined.
- Add the flour mixture and mix till smooth.
- Transfer the mixture into the prepared muffin cups evenly.
- Cook in the oven for about 25-30 minutes or till a toothpick inserted in the center comes out clean.

Amount per serving (12 total)

Timing Information:

Preparation	10 m
Cooking	25 m
Total Time	35 m

Nutritional Information:

Calories	187 kcal
Fat	5.8 g
Carbohydrates	32.3g
Protein	2.6 g
Cholesterol	29 mg
Sodium	275 mg

* Percent Daily Values are based on a 2,000 calorie diet.

SOUTHWESTERN MUFFINS

Ingredients

- 1 C. all-purpose flour
- 1 C. yellow cornmeal
- 1/2 C. white sugar
- 2 tsp baking powder
- 1 tsp salt
- 1 C. buttermilk
- 1/2 C. butter, melted
- 1 egg, beaten

Directions

- Set your oven to 400 degrees F before doing anything else and lightly, grease 12 cups of a muffin pan.
- In a large bowl, mix together the flour, cornmeal, sugar, baking powder and salt.
- Add the buttermilk, butter and egg; mix till well combined.
- Transfer the mixture into the prepared muffin cups evenly.
- Cook in the oven for about 12-15 minutes or till a toothpick inserted in the center comes out clean.
- Remove from the oven and cool for about 15 minutes before turning out onto wire rack to cool completely.

Amount per serving (12 total)

Timing Information:

Preparation	15 m
Cooking	15 m
Total Time	40 m

Nutritional Information:

Calories	195 kcal
Fat	8.6 g
Carbohydrates	26.6g
Protein	3.2 g
Cholesterol	37 mg
Sodium	358 mg

* Percent Daily Values are based on a 2,000 calorie diet.

Thyme Mushroom and Feta Muffins

Ingredients

- cooking spray
- 1 C. cooked quinoa
- 3 large eggs, beaten
- 1/4 C. crumbled feta cheese
- 1/4 C. sliced mushrooms
- 1/4 C. chopped onion
- 1/2 tsp dried thyme
- salt and ground black pepper to taste

Directions

- Set your oven to 400 degrees F before doing anything else and lightly, grease 6 cups of a muffin pan.
- In a large bowl, add the quinoa, eggs, feta cheese, mushrooms, onion, thyme, salt and pepper and beat till well combined.
- Transfer the mixture into the prepared muffin cups about halfway full.
- Cook in the oven for about 20-30 minutes or till a toothpick inserted in the center comes out clean.

Amount per serving (6 total)

Timing Information:

Preparation	15 m
Cooking	20 m
Total Time	35 m

Nutritional Information:

Calories	94 kcal
Fat	4.5 g
Carbohydrates	7.8g
Protein	5.6 g
Cholesterol	99 mg
Sodium	133 mg

* Percent Daily Values are based on a 2,000 calorie diet.

BRITISH FLAT MUFFINS

Ingredients

- 1 C. milk
- 2 tbsp white sugar
- 1 (.25 oz.) package active dry yeast
- 1 C. warm water (110 degrees F/45 degrees C)
- 1/4 C. melted shortening
- 6 C. all-purpose flour
- 1 tsp salt

Directions

- In a small pan, add the milk and warm till bubbles.
- Remove from the heat and add the sugar and cook, stirring continuously till sugar dissolves.
- Remove from the heat and keep aside to cool till lukewarm.
- In a small bowl, dissolve the yeast in warm water and keep aside for about 10 minutes.
- In a large bowl, add the milk, yeast mixture, shortening and 3 C. of the flour and beat till smooth.
- Add the salt and remaining flour and mix till a soft dough forms.

- Knead the dough and place in a greased bowl.
- Cover and keep in warm place to rise.
- Punch down the dough and roll into about 1/2-inch thickness.
- With a biscuit cutter, cut the rounds.
- Sprinkle the cornmeal over a waxed paper and arrange the rounds over it to rise.
- Dust the cornmeal over the tops of muffins.
- Cover and keep in warm place for about 1/2 hour.
- Heat a greased griddle on medium heat and cook the muffins for about 10 minutes per side.
- Keep aside to cool and place in plastic bags for preserving.
- To use, split and toast the muffins.
- Serve with the orange butter, cream cheese or jam.

Amount per serving (18 total)

Timing Information:

Preparation	25 m
Cooking	20 m
Total Time	2 h 15 m

Nutritional Information:

Calories	190 kcal
Fat	3.5 g
Carbohydrates	34g
Protein	4.9 g
Cholesterol	1 mg
Sodium	136 mg

* Percent Daily Values are based on a 2,000 calorie diet.

NORTH AMERICAN STYLE MUFFINS

Ingredients

- 3/4 C. butter
- 1 C. white sugar
- 1 egg
- 3/4 C. milk
- 1 tsp vanilla extract
- 1 3/4 C. sifted all-purpose flour
- 2 1/2 tsp baking powder
- 1/2 tsp salt
- 1 C. huckleberries
- 1 tbsp all-purpose flour

Directions

- Set your oven to 400 degrees F before doing anything else and lightly, grease 15 cups of the muffin pans.
- In a large bowl, add the butter and sugar and beat till creamy and smooth.
- Add the egg, milk and vanilla and mix till well combined.
- In another bowl, mix together 1 3/4 C. of the flour, baking powder and salt.
- Add the flour mixture into egg mixture and mix till just moistened.
- In a bowl, add the huckleberries and remaining flour and toss to coat.
- Fold the huckleberry into the flour mixture.

- Transfer the mixture into the prepared muffin cups about 2/3 full.
- Cook in the oven for about 15 minutes or till a toothpick inserted in the center comes out clean.

Amount per serving (15 total)

Timing Information:

Preparation	15 m
Cooking	15 m
Total Time	30 m

Nutritional Information:

Calories	206 kcal
Fat	10 g
Carbohydrates	27.1g
Protein	2.5 g
Cholesterol	38 mg
Sodium	213 mg

* Percent Daily Values are based on a 2,000 calorie diet.

Japanese Muffins

Ingredients

- cooking spray
- 6 tbsp salted butter, softened
- 1/4 C. chopped seaweed
- 1 1/2 tsp sea salt
- 1 C. all-purpose flour
- 1 C. confectioners' sugar
- 2 eggs
- 3 tbsp honey (optional)
- 1 1/2 tbsp coconut oil
- 1 tbsp ground cinnamon (optional)

Directions

- Set your oven to 375 degrees F before doing anything else and lightly, grease 12 cups of a muffin pan.
- In a bowl, add the butter, seaweed and sea salt and mix till smooth.
- Add the flour, confectioners' sugar, eggs, honey, coconut oil and cinnamon and mix till just combined.
- Transfer the mixture into the prepared muffin cups evenly.
- Cook in the oven for about 12-15 minutes or till a toothpick inserted in the center comes out clean.

Amount per serving (12 total)

Timing Information:

Preparation	10 m
Cooking	15 m
Total Time	25 m

Nutritional Information:

Calories	174 kcal
Fat	8.5 g
Carbohydrates	23.3g
Protein	2.2 g
Cholesterol	46 mg
Sodium	278 mg

* Percent Daily Values are based on a 2,000 calorie diet.

Coconut Brown Sugar Banana Muffins

Ingredients

- 2 tsp coconut oil
- 1/4 C. raisins
- 1 C. warm water
- 1/4 C. coconut oil, softened
- 1/4 C. butter, softened
- 1/2 C. brown sugar
- 2 eggs, beaten
- 2 ripe bananas, mashed
- 4 1/2 oz. applesauce

- 2/3 C. grated carrot
- 1/2 C. bread flour
- 1/2 C. whole-wheat flour
- 1 tbsp ground flax seed
- 1/2 tsp baking soda
- 1/2 tsp salt

- 1/2 tsp vanilla extract

Directions

- Set your oven to 375 degrees F before doing anything else and grease 12 cups of a muffin pan.
- In a bowl of the warm water, soak the raisins for about 10 minutes.
- Drain the raisin and chop them.
- In a bowl, add 1/4 C. of the coconut oil, butter and brown sugar and beat till combined.
- Add the eggs, mashed bananas, applesauce and grated carrot and beat till well combined.

- In another bowl, mix together the bread flour, whole-wheat flour, flax seed, chopped raisins, baking soda, salt and vanilla extract.
- Add the flour mixture into the banana mixture using and gently stir to combine.
- Transfer the mixture into the prepared muffin cups evenly.
- Cook in the oven for about 18 minutes or till a toothpick inserted in the center comes out clean.

Amount per serving (12 total)

Timing Information:

Preparation	15 m
Cooking	18 m
Total Time	43 m

Nutritional Information:

Calories	203 kcal
Fat	10.6 g
Carbohydrates	26g
Protein	3 g
Cholesterol	41 mg
Sodium	197 mg

* Percent Daily Values are based on a 2,000 calorie diet.

November's holiday Muffins

Ingredients

- 1/2 C. sweetened dried cranberries (such as Craisins(R))
- 1 C. hot water, or as needed
- 1 C. whole wheat flour
- 1 C. white sugar
- 1/2 C. oat flour
- 1 tsp baking powder
- 1 tsp baking soda
- 1 tsp salt
- 1 tsp ground cinnamon
- 1/2 tsp ground nutmeg
- 1 (15 oz.) can sweet potatoes, undrained
- 3 eggs
- 1/4 C. coconut oil
- 1/2 C. chopped pecans

Directions

- Set your oven to 350 degrees F before doing anything else and grease 5 cups of a jumbo muffin pan.
- In a bowl of hot water, soak the dried cranberries for about 10 minutes, then drain well.
- In a bowl, add the whole wheat flour, white sugar, oat flour, baking powder, baking soda, salt, cinnamon and nutmeg.
- In another bowl, add the sweet potatoes, eggs and coconut oil and beat till smooth.

- Add the egg mixture into the flour mixture and mix till smooth.
- Fold in the cranberries and pecans.
- Transfer the mixture into the prepared muffin cups evenly.
- Cook in the oven for about 25-30 minutes or till a toothpick inserted in the center comes out clean.

Amount per serving (6 total)

Timing Information:

Preparation	15 m
Cooking	25 m
Total Time	50 m

Nutritional Information:

Calories	505 kcal
Fat	19.7 g
Carbohydrates	78.4g
Protein	8.9 g
Cholesterol	93 mg
Sodium	753 mg

* Percent Daily Values are based on a 2,000 calorie diet.

Restaurant Style Muffins

Ingredients

- 2 C. boiling water
- 5 tsp baking soda
- 5 C. all-purpose flour
- 1 quart buttermilk
- 4 C. bran cereal (such as Kellogg's(R) All-Bran(R))
- 2 C. bran flakes cereal
- 1 C. chopped walnuts
- 1 C. white sugar
- 1/2 C. vegetable oil
- 1/2 C. butter, melted
- 4 eggs, beaten
- 2 tsp ground cinnamon
- 1 tsp salt
- 1/2 tsp ground ginger
- 1/2 tsp nutmeg

Directions

- In a large bowl, mix together the boiling water and baking soda.
- Keep aside to cool slightly.
- Add the flour, buttermilk, bran cereal, bran flakes, walnuts, sugar, oil, butter, eggs, cinnamon, salt, ginger and nutmeg in the baking soda mixture and mix till just combined.
- With a plastic wrap, cover the bowl and refrigerate for at least 8 hours or overnight.

- Set your oven to 375 degrees F before doing anything else and lightly, grease 60 cups of the muffin pans.
- Transfer the mixture into the prepared muffin cups about 1/2 of full.
- Cook in the oven for about 20 minutes or till a toothpick inserted in the center comes out clean.

Amount per serving (60 total)

Timing Information:

Preparation	20 m
Cooking	20 m
Total Time	8 h 40 m

Nutritional Information:

Calories	114 kcal
Fat	5.3 g
Carbohydrates	14.8g
Protein	2.6 g
Cholesterol	17 mg
Sodium	198 mg

* Percent Daily Values are based on a 2,000 calorie diet.

BUTTERMILK APRICOT MUFFINS

Ingredients

- 1 C. chopped dried apricots
- 1 C. boiling water
- 2 C. all-purpose flour
- 3/4 C. white sugar
- 1 tsp baking soda
- 1/2 tsp salt
- 1/4 C. melted butter
- 1/4 C. vegetable oil
- 1 C. buttermilk
- 1 egg

Directions

- Set your oven to 400 degrees F before doing anything else and grease 12 cups of a muffin pan.
- In a bowl, add the apricots and boiling water and keep aside for about 5 minutes.
- In a bowl, mix together the flour, sugar, baking soda and salt.
- In another bowl, add the melted butter, oil, buttermilk and egg and beat till well combined.
- Add the egg mixture into the flour mixture and mix till just moistened.
- Drain the apricots and fold into the mixture.
- Transfer the mixture into the prepared muffin cups evenly.

- Cook in the oven for about 15 minutes or till a toothpick inserted in the center comes out clean.
- Remove from the oven and keep on wire rack to cool completely.

Amount per serving (12 total)

Timing Information:

Preparation	15 m
Cooking	15 m
Total Time	30 m

Nutritional Information:

Calories	238 kcal
Fat	9.2 g
Carbohydrates	36.2g
Protein	3.8 g
Cholesterol	26 mg
Sodium	258 mg

* Percent Daily Values are based on a 2,000 calorie diet.

Healthy Muffins

Ingredients

- 1 1/2 C. wheat bran
- 1 C. buttermilk
- 1/3 C. vegetable oil
- 1 egg
- 2/3 C. brown sugar
- 1/2 tsp vanilla extract
- 1 C. all-purpose flour
- 1 tsp baking soda
- 1 tsp baking powder
- 1/2 tsp salt
- 1/2 C. raisins

Directions

- Set your oven to 375 degrees F before doing anything else and grease 12 cups of a muffin pan.
- In a bowl, mix together the wheat bran and buttermilk and keep aside for about 10 minutes.
- In a second bowl, add the oil, egg, sugar and vanilla and beat till well combined.
- Add the egg mixture into the bran mixture and mix well.
- In a third bowl, sift together flour, baking soda, baking powder and salt.
- Add the flour mixture into the bran mixture and mix till just moistened.
- Fold in the raisins.
- Transfer the mixture into the prepared muffin cups evenly.

- Cook in the oven for about 18-20 minutes or till a toothpick inserted in the center comes out clean.

Amount per serving (12 total)

Timing Information:

Preparation	20 m
Cooking	20 m
Total Time	40 m

Nutritional Information:

Calories	167 kcal
Fat	7.1 g
Carbohydrates	25.6g
Protein	3.5 g
Cholesterol	16 mg
Sodium	262 mg

* Percent Daily Values are based on a 2,000 calorie diet.

BEST BREAKFAST MUFFINS

Ingredients

- 1 1/2 C. all-purpose flour
- 1/2 C. whole wheat flour
- 1 1/4 C. white sugar
- 1 tbsp ground cinnamon
- 2 tsp baking powder
- 1/2 tsp baking soda
- 1/2 tsp salt
- 2 C. grated carrots
- 1 apple - peeled, cored, and chopped
- 1 C. raisins
- 1 egg
- 2 egg whites
- 1/2 C. apple butter
- 1/4 C. vegetable oil
- 1 tbsp vanilla extract
- 2 tbsp chopped walnuts
- 2 tbsp toasted wheat germ

Directions

- Set your oven to 375 degrees F before doing anything else and lightly, grease 18 cups of the muffin pans.
- In a bowl, add the eggs, egg whites, apple butter, oil and vanilla and beat till well combined.
- In another large bowl, mix together the flours, sugar, cinnamon, baking powder, baking soda and salt.
- Add the carrots, apples and raisins and stir to combine.

- Add the egg mixture and mix till just moistened.
- Transfer the mixture into the prepared muffin cups about 3/4 full.
- In a small bowl, mix together the walnuts and wheat germ and sprinkle over the top of muffins.
- Cook in the oven for about 15-20 minutes or till a toothpick inserted in the center comes out clean.

Amount per serving (18 total)

Timing Information:

Preparation	15 m
Cooking	20 m
Total Time	35 m

Nutritional Information:

Calories	194 kcal
Fat	4.2 g
Carbohydrates	37.3g
Protein	3.1 g
Cholesterol	10 mg
Sodium	175 mg

* Percent Daily Values are based on a 2,000 calorie diet.

AUTUMNAL MUFFINS

Ingredients

- 2 1/2 C. all-purpose flour
- 2 C. white sugar
- 1 tbsp pumpkin pie spice
- 1 tsp baking soda
- 1/2 tsp salt
- 2 eggs, lightly beaten
- 1 C. canned pumpkin puree

- 1/2 C. vegetable oil
- 2 C. peeled, cored and chopped apple
- 2 tbsp all-purpose flour
- 1/4 C. white sugar
- 1/2 tsp ground cinnamon
- 4 tsp butter

Directions

- Set your oven to 375 degrees F before doing anything else and lightly, grease 18 cups of the muffin pans.
- In a large bowl, sift together 2 1/2 C. of the all-purpose flour, 2 C. of the sugar, pumpkin pie spice, baking soda and salt.
- In another bowl, add the eggs, pumpkin and oil and beat till well combined.
- Add the pumpkin mixture into the flour mixture and mix till just moistened.
- Fold in the apples.

- Transfer the mixture into the prepared muffin cups evenly.
- In a small bowl, mix together 2 tbsp of the flour, 1/4 C. of the sugar and 1/2 tsp of the cinnamon.
- With a pastry cutter, cut the butter and mix till a coarse crumb forms.
- Sprinkle the crumb mixture over the top of muffins.
- Cook in the oven for about 35-40 minutes or till a toothpick inserted in the center comes out clean.

Amount per serving (18 total)

Timing Information:

Preparation	15 m
Cooking	45 m
Total Time	1 h

Nutritional Information:

Calories	249 kcal
Fat	8 g
Carbohydrates	42.6g
Protein	2.8 g
Cholesterol	23 mg
Sodium	182 mg

* Percent Daily Values are based on a 2,000 calorie diet.

Flax Raisin and Vanilla Muffins

Ingredients

- 1 1/2 C. all-purpose flour
- 3/4 C. ground flax seed
- 3/4 C. oat bran
- 1 C. brown sugar
- 2 tsp baking soda
- 1 tsp baking powder
- 1 tsp salt
- 2 tsp ground cinnamon
- 3/4 C. skim milk
- 2 eggs, beaten
- 1 tsp vanilla extract
- 2 tbsp vegetable oil
- 2 C. shredded carrots
- 2 apples, peeled, shredded
- 1/2 C. raisins
- 1 C. chopped mixed nuts

Directions

- Set your oven to 350 degrees F before doing anything else and grease 15 cups of the muffin pans.
- In a large bowl, mix together the flour, flax seed, oat bran, brown sugar, baking soda, baking powder, salt and cinnamon.
- Add the milk, eggs, vanilla and oil and mix till just moistened.
- Fold in the carrots, apples, raisins and nuts.
- Transfer the mixture into the prepared muffin cups about 2/3 full.

- Cook in the oven for about 15-20 minutes or till a toothpick inserted in the center comes out clean.

Amount per serving (15 total)

Timing Information:

Preparation	15 m
Cooking	20 m
Total Time	35 m

Nutritional Information:

Calories	272 kcal
Fat	11 g
Carbohydrates	40.9g
Protein	6.7 g
Cholesterol	25 mg
Sodium	449 mg

* Percent Daily Values are based on a 2,000 calorie diet.

DUTCH STYLE MUFFINS

Ingredients

- 2 1/4 C. all-purpose flour
- 1 tsp baking soda
- 1/2 tsp salt
- 1 egg
- 1 C. buttermilk
- 1/2 C. butter, melted
- 1 tsp vanilla extract
- 1 1/2 C. packed brown sugar
- 2 C. diced apples
- 1/2 C. packed brown sugar
- 1/3 C. all-purpose flour
- 1 tsp ground cinnamon
- 2 tbsp butter, melted

Directions

- Set your oven to 375 degrees F before doing anything else and lightly, grease 12 cups of a muffin pan.
- In a large bowl, mix together 2 1/4 C. of the flour, baking soda and salt.
- In another smaller bowl, add the egg, buttermilk, 1/2 C. of the melted butter, vanilla and 1 1/2 C. of the brown sugar and beat till sugar dissolves.
- Add the egg mixture and apples into the flour mixture and mix till just combined.
- Transfer the mixture into the prepared muffin cups, filling to the top.

- In a small bowl, mix together 1/2 C. of the brown sugar, 1/3 C. of the flour and cinnamon.
- Drizzle in 2 tbsp of the melted butter while mixing with a fork till well combined.
- Sprinkle the brown sugar mixture over the muffin tops.
- Cook in the oven for about 25 minutes or till a toothpick inserted in the center comes out clean.

Amount per serving (12 total)

Timing Information:

Preparation	15 m
Cooking	25 m
Total Time	40 m

Nutritional Information:

Calories	312 kcal
Fat	10.5 g
Carbohydrates	51.1g
Protein	4.2 g
Cholesterol	42 mg
Sodium	306 mg

* Percent Daily Values are based on a 2,000 calorie diet.

BUTTERMILK BLUEBERRY MUFFINS

Ingredients

- 3/4 C. all-purpose flour
- 3/4 C. whole wheat flour
- 3/4 C. white sugar
- 1/4 C. oat bran
- 1/4 C. quick cooking oats
- 1/4 C. wheat germ
- 1 tsp baking powder
- 1 tsp baking soda
- 1/4 tsp salt

- 1 C. blueberries
- 1/2 C. chopped walnuts
- 1 banana, mashed
- 1 C. buttermilk
- 1 egg
- 1 tbsp vegetable oil
- 1 tsp vanilla extract

Directions

- Set your oven to 350 degrees F before doing anything else and lightly, grease 12 cups of a muffin pan.
- In a large bowl, mix together the flours, sugar, oat bran, quick-cooking oats, wheat germ, baking powder, baking soda and salt.
- Gently, stir in the blueberries and walnuts.
- In another bowl, add the mashed banana, buttermilk, egg, oil and vanilla and beat till well combined.
- Add the egg mixture into the flour mixture and mix till just combined.

- Transfer the mixture into the prepared muffin cups, filling to the top.
- Cook in the oven for about 15-18 minutes or till a toothpick inserted in the center comes out clean.

Amount per serving (12 total)

Timing Information:

Preparation	15 m
Cooking	15 m
Total Time	30 m

Nutritional Information:

Calories	196 kcal
Fat	5.8 g
Carbohydrates	33.4g
Protein	5.1 g
Cholesterol	16 mg
Sodium	223 mg

* Percent Daily Values are based on a 2,000 calorie diet.

Choco-Veggie Muffins

Ingredients

- 1 1/2 C. all-purpose flour
- 3/4 C. white sugar
- 1 tsp baking soda
- 1 tsp ground cinnamon
- 1/2 tsp salt
- 1 egg, lightly beaten
- 1/2 C. vegetable oil
- 1/4 C. milk
- 1 tbsp lemon juice
- 1 tsp vanilla extract
- 1 C. shredded zucchini
- 1/2 C. miniature semisweet chocolate chips
- 1/2 C. chopped walnuts

Directions

- Set your oven to 350 degrees F before doing anything else and lightly, grease 12 cups of a muffin pan.
- In a large bowl, mix together the flour, sugar, baking soda, cinnamon and salt.
- In another bowl, add the egg, oil, milk, lemon juice and vanilla extract and beat till well combined.
- Add the egg mixture into the flour mixture and mix till just moistened.
- Fold in the zucchini, chocolate chips and walnuts.
- Transfer the mixture into the prepared muffin cups about 2/3 full.

- Cook in the oven for about 20-25 minutes or till a toothpick inserted in the center comes out clean.

Amount per serving (12 total)

Timing Information:

Preparation	15 m
Cooking	20 m
Total Time	50 m

Nutritional Information:

Calories	265 kcal
Fat	15.2 g
Carbohydrates	30.6g
Protein	3.5 g
Cholesterol	16 mg
Sodium	212 mg

* Percent Daily Values are based on a 2,000 calorie diet.

September's Pumpkin Muffins

Ingredients

- 1/2 C. raisins
- 1 1/2 C. whole wheat flour
- 1/2 C. packed brown sugar
- 1 tsp pumpkin pie spice
- 3/4 tsp baking powder
- 1/2 tsp baking soda
- 1/2 tsp salt

- 2 eggs
- 3/4 C. canned pumpkin puree
- 1/2 C. vegetable oil
- 1/2 C. honey
- 1/2 C. chopped walnuts

Directions

- Set your oven to 350 degrees F before doing anything else and grease 12 cups of a muffin pan.
- In a bowl of hot water, soak the raisins for a few minutes.
- In a large bowl, stir together the whole wheat flour, brown sugar, pumpkin pie spice, baking powder, baking soda and salt.
- Make a well in the center of the flour mixture.
- In the well, add the eggs, pumpkin, oil and honey and mix till just moistened.
- Drain the raisins completely.
- In the flour mixture, fold in the raisins and walnuts.

- Transfer the mixture into the prepared muffin cups about 2/3 full.
- Cook in the oven for about 18 minutes or till a toothpick inserted in the center comes out clean.
- Remove from the oven and cool before turning out onto wire rack to cool completely.

Amount per serving (12 total)

Timing Information:

Preparation	15 m
Cooking	20 m
Total Time	35 m

Nutritional Information:

Calories	263 kcal
Fat	13 g
Carbohydrates	35.9g
Protein	4.2 g
Cholesterol	31 mg
Sodium	224 mg

* Percent Daily Values are based on a 2,000 calorie diet.

VEGAN CORNMEAL MUFFINS

Ingredients

- 1/2 C. cornmeal
- 1/2 C. whole-wheat pastry flour
- 1/2 tsp baking soda
- 1/2 tsp salt
- 1/2 C. applesauce
- 1/2 C. soy milk
- 1/4 C. agave nectar
- 2 tbsp canola oil

Directions

- Set your oven to 325 degrees F before doing anything else and lightly, grease 6 cups of a muffin pan.
- In a large bowl, mix together the cornmeal, flour, baking soda and salt.
- Add the applesauce, soy milk and agave nectar and stir to combine.
- Slowly add the oil. Stirring continuously till well combined.
- Transfer the mixture into the prepared muffin cups evenly.
- Cook in the oven for about 15-20 minutes or till a toothpick inserted in the center comes out clean.

Amount per serving (6 total)

Timing Information:

Preparation	5 m
Cooking	15 m
Total Time	20 m

Nutritional Information:

Calories	177 kcal
Fat	5.4 g
Carbohydrates	31g
Protein	2.5 g
Cholesterol	0 mg
Sodium	310 mg

* Percent Daily Values are based on a 2,000 calorie diet.

CINNAMON PECAN MUFFINS

Ingredients

- 1 1/2 C. all-purpose flour
- 1/2 C. white sugar
- 1/4 C. brown sugar
- 1 tsp baking soda
- 1 tsp ground cinnamon
- 1/2 tsp salt
- 1/2 C. olive oil
- 1/4 C. milk
- 1 egg
- 1 1/2 tsp vanilla extract
- 1 C. shredded zucchini
- 1/2 C. fresh blueberries
- 1/2 C. chopped pecans

Directions

- Set your oven to 350 degrees F before doing anything else and grease 12 cups of a muffin pan.
- In a bowl, mix together the flour, white sugar, brown sugar, baking soda, cinnamon and salt.
- In another bowl, add the olive oil, milk, egg and vanilla extract and beat till smooth.
- Add the egg mixture into the flour mixture and mix till just moistened.
- Fold in the zucchini, blueberries and pecans.
- Transfer the mixture into the prepared muffin cups about 2/3 full.

- Cook in the oven for about 20-25 minutes or till a toothpick inserted in the center comes out clean.

Amount per serving (12 total)

Timing Information:

Preparation	15 m
Cooking	20 m
Total Time	35 m

Nutritional Information:

Calories	227 kcal
Fat	13 g
Carbohydrates	25.6g
Protein	2.9 g
Cholesterol	16 mg
Sodium	212 mg

* Percent Daily Values are based on a 2,000 calorie diet.

LUNCH BOX MUFFINS

Ingredients

- 1 C. whole wheat flour
- 1/2 C. all-purpose flour
- 3/4 C. white sugar
- 1 1/2 tsp baking powder
- 1/2 tsp salt
- 1/2 C. low-fat vanilla yogurt
- 1/2 C. canola oil
- 1 egg
- 2 tsp vanilla extract
- 1 ripe pear - peeled, cored, and diced
- 1/2 C. chopped pecans

Directions

- Set your oven to 450 degrees F before doing anything else and line 12 cups of a muffin pan with the paper liners.
- In a bowl, mix together the flours, sugar, baking powder and salt.
- In another bowl, add the yogurt, oil, egg and vanilla extract and beat till smooth.
- Add the yogurt mixture into the flour mixture and mix till just combined.
- Fold in the pear and pecans.
- Transfer the mixture into the prepared muffin cups evenly.

- Place the muffin pan in the oven and immediately, set it to 350 degrees F.
- Cook in the oven for about 20-25 minutes or till a toothpick inserted in the center comes out clean.
- Remove from the oven and cool for about 5 minutes before turning out onto wire rack to cool completely.

Amount per serving (12 total)

Timing Information:

Preparation	15 m
Cooking	20 m
Total Time	1 h

Nutritional Information:

Calories	240 kcal
Fat	13.4 g
Carbohydrates	28.2g
Protein	3.4 g
Cholesterol	16 mg
Sodium	171 mg

* Percent Daily Values are based on a 2,000 calorie diet.

Honey Almond Muffins

Ingredients

- 2 eggs, separated
- 2 tbsp margarine, softened
- 2 tbsp honey
- 1/4 tsp almond extract
- 1/3 C. boiling water
- 3/4 C. unsweetened flaked coconut
- 3/4 C. all-purpose flour

Directions

- Set your oven to 350 degrees F before doing anything else and grease 12 cups of a muffin pan.
- In a large bowl add the egg yolks and beat.
- Add the butter, honey, almond extract, boiling water, coconut and flour and mix till just combined.
- In another bowl, add the egg whites and with an electric mixer, beat till stiff.
- Fold the egg whites into the flour mixture.
- Transfer the mixture into the prepared muffin cups about 2/3 full.
- Cook in the oven for about 20-25 minutes or till a toothpick inserted in the center comes out clean.

Amount per serving (12 total)

Timing Information:

Preparation	10 m
Cooking	30 m
Total Time	50 m

Nutritional Information:

Calories	107 kcal
Fat	6.6 g
Carbohydrates	10.3g
Protein	2.3 g
Cholesterol	31 mg
Sodium	40 mg

* Percent Daily Values are based on a 2,000 calorie diet.

CARIBBEAN ROLLED OATS MUFFINS

Ingredients

- 1 C. water
- 1/2 C. rolled oats
- 1 1/2 C. all-purpose flour
- 1/4 C. wheat bran
- 1/3 C. white sugar
- 4 tsp baking powder
- 1/8 tsp ground nutmeg
- 1 mashed banana
- 1 beaten egg
- 1 (8 oz.) can crushed pineapple, well drained
- 1 C. coconut milk
- 1/8 tsp coconut extract

Directions

- In a pan, add the water and bring to a boil.
- Stir in the oats and cook for about 1 minute.
- Cover and remove from the heat, then keep aside to cool.
- Set your oven to 375 degrees F before doing anything else and grease and flour 12 cups of a muffin pan.
- In a large bowl, mix together the flour, bran, sugar, baking powder and nutmeg.
- Make a well in the center of the mixture.
- In the well, add the mashed banana, cooled oatmeal, egg, pineapple, coconut milk and coconut extract and mix till smooth.

- Transfer the mixture into the prepared muffin cups evenly.
- Cook in the oven for about 25-30 minutes or till a toothpick inserted in the center comes out clean.

Amount per serving (12 total)

Timing Information:

Preparation	15 m
Cooking	30 m
Total Time	45 m

Nutritional Information:

Calories	158 kcal
Fat	4.9 g
Carbohydrates	26.6g
Protein	3.3 g
Cholesterol	16 mg
Sodium	129 mg

* Percent Daily Values are based on a 2,000 calorie diet.

Molasses and Allspice Muffins

Ingredients

- 2 C. whole wheat flour
- 2 C. all-purpose flour
- 2 tbsp baking powder
- 1 tsp salt
- 1/2 C. packed brown sugar
- 1 tsp ground cinnamon
- 1/4 tsp ground allspice
- 2 C. finely grated carrots
- 2 eggs
- 2 C. milk
- 1/2 C. molasses
- 1/2 C. melted butter
- 1 C. chopped walnuts
- 1 C. raisins

Directions

- Set your oven to 400 degrees F before doing anything else and lightly, grease 24 cups of the muffin pans.
- In a large bowl, mix together the flours, baking powder, salt, brown sugar, cinnamon, allspice and grated carrots.
- In another bowl beat the eggs.
- Add the milk, molasses and butter and mix till well combined.
- Add the egg mixture into the flour mixture and mix till just moistened.
- Fold in the walnuts and raisins.
- Transfer the mixture into the prepared muffin cups evenly.

- Cook in the oven for about 25-30 minutes or till a toothpick inserted in the center comes out clean.

Amount per serving (24 total)

Timing Information:

Preparation	10 m
Cooking	30 m
Total Time	45 m

Nutritional Information:

Calories	214 kcal
Fat	8.2 g
Carbohydrates	32.5g
Protein	4.7 g
Cholesterol	27 mg
Sodium	272 mg

* Percent Daily Values are based on a 2,000 calorie diet.

I ♥ Muffins

Ingredients

- 2 C. all-purpose flour
- 3 tsp baking powder
- 1/2 tsp salt
- 1/2 C. white sugar

- 1 egg, beaten
- 3/4 C. milk
- 1/4 C. vegetable oil
- 1 C. any flavor fruit jam

Directions

- Set your oven to 400 degrees F before doing anything else and line 12 cups of a muffin pan with the paper liners
- In a large bowl, mix together the flour, baking powder, salt and sugar.
- Make a well in the center of the flour mixture.
- In another bowl, add the egg, milk and oil and beat till well combined.
- Add the egg mixture in the well of flour mixture and mix till just moistened.
- Gently stir in the jam.
- Transfer the mixture into the prepared muffin cups evenly.
- Cook in the oven for about 25 minutes or till a toothpick inserted in the center comes out clean.

Amount per serving (12 total)

Timing Information:

Preparation	10 m
Cooking	30 m
Total Time	40 m

Nutritional Information:

Calories	236 kcal
Fat	5.5 g
Carbohydrates	43.5g
Protein	3.3 g
Cholesterol	17 mg
Sodium	240 mg

* Percent Daily Values are based on a 2,000 calorie diet.

BROWN SUGAR BISCUIT MUFFINS

Ingredients

- 1 tsp apple pie spice
- 1/4 C. white sugar
- 1 (12 oz.) can refrigerated biscuit dough, separated and cut into six pieces
- 1/2 C. brown sugar
- 3 tbsp butter
- 1 tsp water

Directions

- Set your oven to 375 degrees F before doing anything else and lightly, grease 12 cups of a muffin pan.
- In a bowl, mix together the apple pie spice and white sugar.
- Add the biscuit pieces and roll to coat.
- Divide the coated biscuit dough pieces into the prepared muffin cups.
- In a small pan, mix together the brown sugar, butter, and water on medium heat and bring to a boil, stirring continuously.
- Boil, stirring continuously for about 2-3 minutes.
- Place the butter mixture over the biscuit pieces evenly.
- Cook in the oven for about 8-12 minutes or till a toothpick inserted in the center comes out clean.

Amount per serving (6 total)

Timing Information:

Preparation	10 m
Cooking	15 m
Total Time	25 m

Nutritional Information:

Calories	313 kcal
Fat	13.5 g
Carbohydrates	45g
Protein	3.9 g
Cholesterol	16 mg
Sodium	612 mg

* Percent Daily Values are based on a 2,000 calorie diet.

TROPICAL MUFFINS

Ingredients

- 1 1/2 C. all-purpose flour
- 1 tsp baking soda
- 1 tsp baking powder
- 1/2 tsp salt
- 3 bananas, mashed
- 3/4 C. white sugar
- 1/3 C. butter, melted
- 1 egg, beaten
- 1 tbsp rum-flavored extract
- 1 tsp vanilla extract
- 1/2 (20 oz.) can pineapple chunks, drained
- 3/4 C. shredded unsweetened coconut, divided

Directions

- Set your oven to 350 degrees F before doing anything else and grease 12 cups of a muffin pan.
- In a large bowl, sift together the flour, baking soda, baking powder and salt.
- In another bowl, add the bananas, sugar, butter, egg, rum-flavored extract and vanilla extract and beat till well combined.
- Add the flour mixture, 1 C. at a time into the banana mixture and mix till well combined.
- Gently, fold in the pineapple chunks and 1/2 C. of the coconut.

- Transfer the mixture into the prepared muffin cups evenly and sprinkle with the remaining shredded coconut.
- Cook in the oven for about 25-30 minutes or till a toothpick inserted in the center comes out clean.
- Remove from the oven and cool for about 10 minutes before turning out onto wire rack to cool completely.

Amount per serving (12 total)

Timing Information:

Preparation	15 m
Cooking	25 m
Total Time	50 m

Nutritional Information:

Calories	239 kcal
Fat	9.5 g
Carbohydrates	36.4g
Protein	3 g
Cholesterol	29 mg
Sodium	288 mg

[x] Percent Daily Values are based on a 2,000 calorie diet.

CEREAL MUFFINS

Ingredients

- 6 C. boiling water
- 6 C. whole bran cereal
- 3 C. margarine
- 9 C. white sugar
- 12 eggs

- 12 C. buttermilk
- 15 C. all-purpose flour
- 5 tbsp baking soda
- 1 tbsp salt
- 12 C. whole bran cereal

Directions

- In a larger bowl, mix together the boiling water and 6 C. of the bran cereal.
- Keep aside to cool.
- Set your oven to 425 degrees F and line the cups of the muffin pans with the paper liners.
- In another bowl, add the margarine, sugar, eggs, and buttermilk and beat till well combined.
- Add the egg mixture into the bran mixture and stir to combine.
- Add the flour, baking soda and salt and stir to combine.
- Add 12 C. of the bran cereal and mix till just moistened.
- Transfer the mixture into the prepared muffin cups in the batches.

- Cook in the oven for about 20-25 minutes or till a toothpick inserted in the center comes out clean.

Amount per serving (216 total)

Timing Information:

Preparation	10 m
Cooking	30 m
Total Time	40 m

Nutritional Information:

Calories	106 kcal
Fat	3.4 g
Carbohydrates	17.6g
Protein	1.9 g
Cholesterol	11 mg
Sodium	150 mg

* Percent Daily Values are based on a 2,000 calorie diet.

WHOLESOME MUFFINS

Ingredients

- 1/3 C. whole wheat flour
- 1/3 C. soy flour
- 1/3 C. rye flour
- 1 tsp baking powder
- 1 tsp baking soda
- 1/2 tsp salt
- 1 tbsp vegetable oil
- 1 egg, beaten
- 1 C. buttermilk
- 1 tbsp molasses

Directions

- Set your oven to 375 degrees F before doing anything else and lightly, grease 12 cups of a muffin pan.
- In a large bowl, mix together the flours, baking powder, baking soda and salt.
- With a fork, stir in the oil.
- Add egg, buttermilk and molasses and mix till well combined
- Transfer the mixture into the prepared muffin cups evenly.
- Cook in the oven for about 17 minutes or till a toothpick inserted in the center comes out clean.

Amount per serving (8 total)

Timing Information:

Preparation	10 m
Cooking	30 m
Total Time	40 mm

Nutritional Information:

Calories	92 kcal
Fat	3.5 g
Carbohydrates	11.8g
Protein	4 g
Cholesterol	24 mg
Sodium	406 mg

* Percent Daily Values are based on a 2,000 calorie diet.

Buttermilk Bran Muffins

Ingredients

- 5 C. all-purpose flour
- 4 C. bran flakes cereal
- 3 C. white sugar
- 5 tsp baking soda
- 2 tsp salt

- 4 eggs, beaten
- 1 C. melted shortening, cooled
- 4 C. buttermilk

Directions

- In a large bowl, sift together the flour.
- Add the cereal, sugar, baking soda and salt and stir to combine.
- Add eggs, shortening and buttermilk and mix till well combined.
- Cover the bowl and refrigerator for at least 24 hours before using.
- Set your oven to 400 degrees F and lightly, grease 48 cups of the muffin pans.
- Transfer the mixture into the prepared muffin cups about 2/3 full.
- Cook in the oven for about 15-20 minutes or till a toothpick inserted in the center comes out clean.

Amount per serving (48 total)

Timing Information:

Preparation	15 m
Cooking	20 m
Total Time	1 d 1 h

Nutritional Information:

Calories	155 kcal
Fat	5 g
Carbohydrates	25.4g
Protein	2.8 g
Cholesterol	16 mg
Sodium	273 mg

* Percent Daily Values are based on a 2,000 calorie diet.

OATS AND CINNAMON MUFFINS

Ingredients

- 2 C. quick-cooking oats
- 2 C. buttermilk
- 2 eggs, beaten
- 1 C. packed brown sugar
- 1/2 C. butter, melted
- 2 C. all-purpose flour
- 2 tsp baking powder
- 1 tsp baking soda
- 1 tsp ground cinnamon
- 1 tsp salt

Directions

- Set your oven to 400 degrees F before doing anything else and grease 24 cups of the muffin pans.
- In a large bowl, mix together the oats and buttermilk and keep aside for about 15 minutes.
- In a bowl, add the eggs, brown sugar and butter and beat till well combined.
- Add the egg mixture into the oat mixture and stir to combine.
- In another bowl, mix together the flour, baking powder, baking soda, cinnamon and salt.
- Add the flour mixture into the oat mixture and mix till just moistened.
- Transfer the mixture into the prepared muffin cups about 3/4 full.

- Cook in the oven for about 15-18 minutes or till a toothpick inserted in the center comes out clean.
- Remove from the oven and cool for about 10 minutes before turning out onto wire rack to cool completely.

Amount per serving (24 total)

Timing Information:

Preparation	15 m
Cooking	15 m
Total Time	1 h 15 m

Nutritional Information:

Calories	147 kcal
Fat	5 g
Carbohydrates	22.7g
Protein	3.2 g
Cholesterol	26 mg
Sodium	248 mg

* Percent Daily Values are based on a 2,000 calorie diet.

GEORGIAN MUFFINS

Ingredients

- 3 C. all-purpose flour
- 1 tbsp ground cinnamon
- 1 tsp baking soda
- 1 tsp salt
- 1 1/4 C. vegetable oil
- 3 eggs, lightly beaten
- 2 C. white sugar
- 2 C. peeled, pitted, and chopped peaches

Directions

- Set your oven to 400 degrees F before doing anything else and lightly, grease 16 cups of the muffin pans.
- In a large bowl, mix together the flour, cinnamon, baking soda and salt.
- In another bowl, add the oil, eggs and sugar and beat till smooth.
- Add the oil mixture into the flour mixture and mix till just moistened.
- Fold in the peaches.
- Transfer the mixture into the prepared muffin cups evenly.
- Cook in the oven for about 25 minutes or till a toothpick inserted in the center comes out clean.
- Remove from the oven and cool for about 10 minutes before turning out onto wire rack to cool completely.

Amount per serving (16 total)

Timing Information:

Preparation	25 m
Cooking	25 m
Total Time	50 m

Nutritional Information:

Calories	351 kcal
Fat	18.2 g
Carbohydrates	44.3g
Protein	3.6 g
Cholesterol	35 mg
Sodium	238 mg

* Percent Daily Values are based on a 2,000 calorie diet.

CITRUS BOOST MUFFINS

Ingredients

- 2 C. all-purpose flour
- 1/2 C. white sugar
- 3 tsp baking powder
- 1/2 tsp salt
- 3/4 C. orange juice
- 1/3 C. vegetable oil
- 1 egg
- 1 tbsp orange zest

Directions

- Set your oven to 400 degrees F before doing anything else and lightly, grease 12 cups of a muffin pan.
- In a bowl, mix together the flour, sugar, baking powder, orange peel and salt.
- In another bowl, add the orange juice, oil and egg and beat till well combined.
- Add the flour mixture and mix till just moistened.
- Transfer the mixture into the prepared muffin cups about 2/3 full.
- Cook in the oven for about 20-25 minutes or till a toothpick inserted in the center comes out clean.

Amount per serving (12 total)

Timing Information:

Preparation	10 m
Cooking	30 m
Total Time	40 m

Nutritional Information:

Calories	176 kcal
Fat	6.8 g
Carbohydrates	26.3g
Protein	2.8 g
Cholesterol	16 mg
Sodium	225 mg

* Percent Daily Values are based on a 2,000 calorie diet.

MEAT MUFFINS

Ingredients

- 2 lb. lean ground beef
- 1 (10.5 oz.) can condensed vegetable soup
- 1/2 C. chopped onion
- 1 C. dry bread crumbs
- 2 eggs
- 1 tsp salt
- 1 pinch ground black pepper
- 3/4 C. ketchup (optional)

Directions

- Set your oven to 350 degrees F before doing anything else and lightly, grease 12 cups of a muffin pan.
- In a large bowl, add the ground beef, soup, onion, bread crumbs, eggs, salt and pepper and mix till well combined.
- Transfer the mixture into the prepared muffin cups evenly.
- Set the oven to 160 degrees F just before placing the muffin pan inside.
- Cook in the oven for about 50 minutes.
- Remove the muffin pan from the oven and top each muffin with the ketchup.
- Cook in the oven for about 10 minutes more.

Amount per serving (6 total)

Timing Information:

Preparation	15 m
Cooking	1 h
Total Time	1 h 15 m

Nutritional Information:

Calories	464 kcal
Fat	22.7 g
Carbohydrates	26.9g
Protein	36.9 g
Cholesterol	165 mg
Sodium	1285 mg

[x] Percent Daily Values are based on a 2,000 calorie diet.

HASH BROWN BREAKFAST MUFFINS

Ingredients

- 12 links Johnsonville(R) Original breakfast sausage
- 3 C. frozen country style shredded hash brown potatoes, thawed
- 3 tbsp butter, melted
- 1/8 tsp salt
- 1/8 tsp pepper
- 6 eggs, lightly beaten
- 2 C. shredded 4-cheese Mexican blend cheese
- 1/4 C. chopped red bell pepper
- chopped fresh chives

Directions

- Set your oven to 400 degrees F before doing anything else and grease 12 cups of a muffin pan.
- Prepare the sausage according to the package's directions.
- Keep aside to cool slightly and cut into 1/2-inch pieces.
- In a bowl, mix together the hash browns, butter, salt and pepper.
- Transfer the mixture into the prepared muffin cups evenly and press onto the sides and bottom of the cups.
- Cook in the oven for about 12 minutes.

- Remove from the oven and divide the sausage pieces into muffin cups evenly.
- In a bowl, mix together the eggs, cheese and bell pepper.
- Place the egg mixture into muffin cups and top with the chives.
- Cook in the oven for about 13-15 minutes more.

Amount per serving (12 total)

Timing Information:

Preparation	20 m
Cooking	30 m
Total Time	50 m

Nutritional Information:

Calories	224 kcal
Fat	18.3 g
Carbohydrates	8.6g
Protein	11.2 g
Cholesterol	114 mg
Sodium	413 mg

* Percent Daily Values are based on a 2,000 calorie diet.

Beef Mushroom Muffins

Ingredients

- 3 tbsp butter, softened
- 12 slices white bread
- 1 1/4 lb. ground beef
- 1 egg
- 1 small onion, chopped
- 1 (10.75 oz.) can condensed cream of mushroom soup
- salt and pepper to taste
- 3/4 C. shredded Cheddar cheese

Directions

- Set your oven to 350 degrees F before doing anything else.
- Spread the butter over one side of each bread slice.
- Arrange each bread slice, butter-side down into the cups of a muffin pan and press.
- In a medium bowl, add the ground beef, egg, onion, cream of mushroom soup, salt and pepper and mix till well combined.
- Fill each bread cup with the beef mixture evenly and sprinkle with the shredded Cheddar cheese.
- Cook in the oven for about 30 minutes.

Amount per serving (12 total)

Timing Information:

Preparation	15 m
Cooking	30 m
Total Time	45 m

Nutritional Information:

Calories	303 kcal
Fat	21 g
Carbohydrates	15g
Protein	12.9 g
Cholesterol	72 mg
Sodium	446 mg

* Percent Daily Values are based on a 2,000 calorie diet.

Burger Muffins

Ingredients

- cooking spray
- 1 lb. ground beef
- 1 small onion, chopped
- 2 1/2 C. all-purpose flour
- 1 tbsp white sugar
- 2 tsp baking powder
- 1 tsp salt
- 3/4 C. ketchup
- 3/4 C. milk
- 1/2 C. butter, melted
- 2 eggs, beaten
- 1 tsp prepared yellow mustard
- 2 C. shredded Cheddar cheese

Directions

- Set your oven to 425 degrees F before doing anything else and line 24 cups of the muffin pans with lightly, greased paper liners.
- Heat a large skillet on medium-high heat and cook the beef and onion for about 5-7 minutes.
- Discard the grease.
- In a large bowl, mix together the flour, sugar, baking powder and salt.
- In another bowl, mix together the ketchup, milk, butter, eggs and mustard.

- Add the ketchup mixture into the flour mixture and stir till a pink color forms.
- Add the cooked ground beef mixture and mix till combined.
- Transfer the mixture into the prepared muffin cups evenly.
- Cook in the oven for about 30-40 minutes or till a toothpick inserted in the center comes out clean.
- Remove from the oven and cool for about 10 minutes before turning out onto wire rack to cool completely.

Amount per serving (24 total)

Timing Information:

Preparation	20 m
Cooking	45 m
Total Time	1 h 5 m

Nutritional Information:

Calories	174 kcal
Fat	10 g
Carbohydrates	13.2g
Protein	7.9 g
Cholesterol	48 mg
Sodium	329 mg

* Percent Daily Values are based on a 2,000 calorie diet.

COCONUT CAKE MUFFINS

Ingredients

- 2 1/4 C. all-purpose flour
- 1 tbsp baking powder
- 2 tsp ground cinnamon
- 1/4 tsp ground nutmeg
- 1/4 tsp ground allspice
- 1/4 tsp salt
- 1 C. brown sugar
- 2/3 C. white sugar
- 1 C. flaked coconut
- 2 eggs
- 1/2 C. vegetable oil
- 1/2 C. buttermilk
- 3 carrots, grated
- 1 (8 oz.) can crushed pineapple, with juice
- 1 tbsp vanilla extract
- 1 C. sifted confectioners' sugar
- 1 tsp ground cinnamon
- 2 tbsp buttermilk

Directions

- Set your oven to 375 degrees F before doing anything else and lightly, grease 12 cups of 2 muffin pans.
- In a large bowl, mix together the flour, baking powder, 2 tsp of the cinnamon, 1/4 tsp of the nutmeg, allspice, salt, brown sugar, white sugar and coconut.

- In another bowl, mix together the eggs, oil, 1/2 C. of the buttermilk, carrots, pineapple and vanilla.
- Make a well in the center of the flour mixture.
- Add the egg mixture and mix till just moistened.
- Transfer the mixture into the prepared muffin cups about 3/4 full.
- Cook in the oven for about 20-25 minutes or till a toothpick inserted in the center comes out clean.
- Remove from the oven and keep onto wire rack to cool.
- Meanwhile in a small bowl, add the confectioners' sugar, 1 tsp of the cinnamon and 2-3 tbsp of the buttermilk and mix till smooth.
- Refrigerate till thickened.
- Drizzle over the cooled muffins and serve.

Amount per serving (24 total)

Timing Information:

Preparation	15 m
Cooking	20 m
Total Time	35 m

Nutritional Information:

Calories	193 kcal
Fat	6 g
Carbohydrates	33.3g
Protein	2.2 g
Cholesterol	16 mg
Sodium	96 mg

* Percent Daily Values are based on a 2,000 calorie diet.

FALL SEASON APPLE MUFFINS

Ingredients

- 2 1/2 C. all-purpose flour
- 2 C. white sugar
- 1 tbsp pumpkin pie spice
- 1 tsp baking soda
- 1/2 tsp salt
- 2 eggs, lightly beaten
- 1 C. canned pumpkin puree
- 1/2 C. vegetable oil
- 2 C. peeled, cored and chopped apple
- 2 tbsp all-purpose flour
- 1/4 C. white sugar
- 1/2 tsp ground cinnamon
- 4 tsp butter

Directions

- Set your oven to 350 degrees F before doing anything else and lightly, grease 18 cups of muffin trays.
- In a large bowl, sift together 2 1/2 C. of the flour, baking soda, 2 C. of the sugar, pumpkin pie spice and salt.
- In another bowl, add the eggs, oil and pumpkin and beat till well combined.
- Add the egg mixture into the flour mixture and mix till well combined.
- Fold in the apples and transfer the mixture onto the prepared muffin cups evenly.

- In another bowl, mix together the remaining flour, sugar and cinnamon.
- With a pastry cutter, cut the butter and mix till a coarse crumb forms.
- Place the mixture over each muffin evenly and cook everything in the oven for about 35-40 minutes or till a toothpick inserted in the center comes out clean.

Amount per serving (18 total)

Timing Information:

Preparation	15 m
Cooking	45 m
Total Time	1 h

Nutritional Information:

Calories	249 kcal
Fat	8 g
Carbohydrates	42.6g
Protein	2.8 g
Cholesterol	23 mg
Sodium	182 mg

* Percent Daily Values are based on a 2,000 calorie diet.

PHENOMENAL CRACKER MUFFINS

Ingredients

- 2 1/2 C. graham cracker crumbs
- 1/4 C. white sugar
- 2 tsp baking powder
- 1 C. whole milk
- 1 egg, slightly beaten
- 2 tbsp honey

Directions

- Set your oven to 400 degrees F before doing anything else and grease 10 C. of a muffin tin.
- In a bowl, mix together the cracker crumbs, sugar and baking powder.
- Add the egg, milk and honey and mix till well combined.
- Place the mixture into the prepared muffin tin.
- Cook everything in the oven for about 15-18 minutes or till a toothpick inserted in the center comes out clean.
- Remove everything from the oven and keep aside to cool completely.

Amount per serving (10 total)

Timing Information:

Preparation	10 m
Cooking	18 m
Total Time	30 m

Nutritional Information:

Calories	143 kcal
Fat	3.4 g
Carbohydrates	25.9g
Protein	2.9 g
Cholesterol	21 mg
Sodium	216 mg

* Percent Daily Values are based on a 2,000 calorie diet.

Grape Muffins for a Sweet Day

Ingredients

- 2 1/2 C. flour
- 1 C. sugar
- 2 1/2 tsp baking powder
- 1 C. milk
- 1 tsp vanilla

- 2 eggs, well beaten
- 1/2 C. butter, melted
- 1 1/2 C. red seedless grapes, cut into pieces

Directions

- Set your oven to 375 degrees F before doing anything else and line 12 cups of a muffin tin with paper liners.
- In a large bowl, mix together the flour, baking powder and sugar.
- Make a well in the center of the flour mixture and add the eggs, milk, butter and vanilla and mix till well combined.
- Fold in the grapes and transfer the mixture into prepared muffin cups.
- Cook everything in the oven for about 25 minutes.

Amount per serving: 12

Timing Information:

Preparation	15 mins
Total Time	40 mins

Nutritional Information:

Calories	266.5
Fat	9.4g
Cholesterol	54.1mg
Sodium	166.0mg
Carbohydrates	41.2g
Protein	4.6g

* Percent Daily Values are based on a 2,000 calorie diet.

MASS ZESTY MUFFINS

Ingredients

- 1 1/2 C. all-purpose flour
- 3 tsps baking powder
- Salt, to taste
- 1/4 C. vegetable oil
- 1/4 C. white sugar

- 1 egg
- 1 C. fresh orange juice
- 1 1/2 C. cranberries, chopped
- 1 tbsp fresh orange zest, grated finely

Directions:

- Set your oven to 400 degrees before doing anything else.
- Grease and flour a 12 C. muffin tin.
- In a large bowl, mix together the flour, baking powder and salt.
- In another bowl, add the oil and sugar and beat till light.
- Add the egg and orange juice and beat till well combined.
- Add the egg mixture into the flour mixture and mix till well combined also.
- Fold in the cranberries and orange zest.
- Place the mixture into the prepared muffin C. about 2/3 of full.
- Bake everything for about 20-25 minutes or till a toothpick inserted in the center comes out clean.

Amount per serving (12 total)

Timing Information:

Preparation	10 m
Cooking	30 m
Total Time	40 m

Nutritional Information:

Calories	136 kcal
Fat	5.2 g
Carbohydrates	20.4g
Protein	2.3 g
Cholesterol	16 mg
Sodium	177 mg

* Percent Daily Values are based on a 2,000 calorie diet.

Springtime Muffins

Ingredients

- 2 C. all-purpose flour
- 2 tsps baking powder
- Salt, to taste
- 1 1/2 C. white sugar, divided
- 1/2 C. butter, softened
- 2 eggs
- 1/4 C. milk
- 1/2 C. fresh blueberries, mashed
- 2 C. fresh blueberries

Directions:

- Set your oven to 375 degrees before doing anything else.
- Grease and flour an 18 C. muffin tin.
- In a large bowl, mix together the flour, baking powder and salt.
- In another bowl, add 1 1/4 C. of sugar and butter and beat till light.
- Add the eggs, one at a time and beat till well combined.
- Add the egg mixture into the flour mixture and mix till well combined.
- Add the milk and mix well.
- Add the mashed blueberries and mix well.
- Fold in the fresh blueberries.
- Place the mixture into prepared muffin C. so that about 2/3 of each section is full.

- Dust with the remaining sugar.
- Bake everything for about 30 minutes or till a toothpick inserted in the center comes out clean.

Amount per serving (18 total)

Timing Information:

Preparation	10 m
Cooking	40 m
Total Time	50 m

Nutritional Information:

Calories	182 kcal
Fat	5.9 g
Carbohydrates	30.5g
Protein	2.4 g
Cholesterol	34 mg
Sodium	165 mg

* Percent Daily Values are based on a 2,000 calorie diet.

Thanks for Reading! Join the Club and Keep on Cooking with 6 More Cookbooks....

http://bit.ly/1TdrStv

 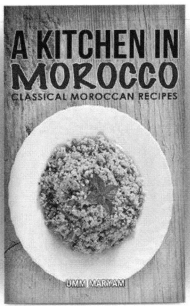 

To grab the box sets simply follow the link mentioned above, or tap one of book covers.

This will take you to a page where you can simply enter your email address and a PDF version of the box sets will be emailed to you.

Hope you are ready for some serious cooking!

http://bit.ly/1TdrStv

COME ON...
LET'S BE FRIENDS :)

We adore our readers and love connecting with them socially.

Like BookSumo on Facebook and let's get social!

Facebook

And also check out the BookSumo Cooking Blog.

Food Lover Blog

Printed in Great Britain
by Amazon